Action Replay

A Play

Fay Weldon

Samuel French – London
New York – Sydney – Toronto – Hollywood

ACTION REPLAY

Characters:

Helen
Judy
Shirley
Saul
Stephen
Jonathan

The action of the play takes place in a flat shared by the three girls, and elsewhere

Time—1952 to 1977

Action Replay was first performed at the Birmingham Repertory Studio Theatre in February 1979.

PLAYSET

PRODUCTION NOTE

The stage can be empty, except for a few props—see Furniture and Property List, p. 40.

The passage of time—1952 to 1977—can be indicated, by the women, by the changing of a skirt or a wig: the men can put ties and sideboards on or off, or ignore the problem altogether.

ACT I

A flat. 1952

The flat is shared by Helen, Shirley and Judy. All three girls are students. Helen is willowy, lovely and difficult; Shirley is pretty and prosaic; Judy is plain, tough and sexy

Saul is escorting Helen home to the flat. He is Jewish, conventional and ambitious, and is at an architectural college. Helen is driving him mad, as girls in the nineteen-fifties drove young men mad. She lets him kiss her, outside the door, then pushes him away. Judy and Shirley, meanwhile, are sitting in the flat, with their books

Saul Can't I come in?

Helen No.

Saul Not even for coffee?

Helen We haven't any coffee. We're all on grants.

Saul Tea.

Helen It would only keep you awake.

Saul Please let me come in.

Helen No. I'm sure your mother's staying up for you. You ought to go home, put her out of her misery. Thank you for dinner and the show. It must have been very expensive.

Saul It was.

Helen You needn't have got such good seats. We could have gone in the gods.

Saul You wouldn't have come out with me again.

Helen No. That's true.

Saul Let me kiss you again.

Helen All right. But keep your hands to yourself . . .

Saul You have such lovely breasts . . .

Helen You don't buy me, you know, by taking me out.

Saul I love you. That's its own reward. I respect you. You just drive me mad. Helen, it hurts—please let me come in for coffee.

Helen You're some kind of animal—leave me alone—you frighten me— you're disgusting—animal!

He turns on his heel, offended, and leaves; then comes back and they play the scene again—they kiss

Saul Can't I come in?

Helen No.

Saul Not even for coffee?

Helen We haven't any coffee. We're all on grants.

Saul Tea.
Helen It would only keep you awake.
Saul Please let me come in.
Helen No. I'm sure your mother's staying up for you.
Saul Of course she isn't.
Helen Yes she is. She's having kittens. You're a good Jewish boy and I'm a shiksa girl.
Saul It's because I'm Jewish, isn't it. I'm good enough to take you out and spend money on you, but not good enough to come back after the show for a cup of coffee. Are you afraid of what your friends will say? Is that it?
Helen Yes, actually. That's perfectly true. You're just not my kind. I'm waiting my time.

Helen goes inside and shuts the door: Shirley and Judy look up from their books briefly: look down again as she goes out of the door, back to Saul, and they play the scene again. They kiss

Saul Can't I come in?
Helen No.
Saul Not even for coffee?
Helen We haven't any coffee. We're all on grants.
Saul Tea.
Helen It would only keep you awake.
Saul Please let me come in.
Helen No. I'm sure your mother's staying up for you. You ought to go home. Put her out of her misery. Thank you for dinner and the show. It must have been very expensive.
Saul I don't think of money when I'm with you. I don't care what happens next. When can I see you again? Helen, let me come in. You've got your friends to chaperone you. I promise I won't make a move out of place. I respect you too much. I think of you day and night, that's all. My finals are coming up—I can't concentrate. I feel you're angry with me. Are you?
Helen No. I've had a lovely evening, that's all. I don't want it spoiled. Someone might see. I could get thrown out of college.
Saul I only want a cup of tea, Helen. Just to sit for a little and look at you, as if—I promise I won't—I apologize most sincerely. I was just carried away for a moment. You're so lovely, Helen. Please.
Helen All right. Come in. Just for half-an-hour.

They both go inside. Shirley and Judy stand to be introduced

Shirley, Judy, this is Saul King. He's Stephen's brother. You know Stephen—Jonathan's friend. You know Jonathan, the anaesthetist at Charing Cross.
Judy Yes I know Jonathan; he's always drunk. If you ever get taken ill, Saul, never go to Charing Cross. They're all drunk.
Shirley That wasn't drink. That was food poisoning. He told me the next day: he'd eaten oysters.
Helen Jonathan could afford oysters?

Shirley Saul, you've got a rival. Helen's an oysters and champagne girl.
Helen That's not fair. I just don't see any point in living badly when you can live well.
Judy Of course her face is her fortune. Personally, I have to rely on my brains. My bad luck. Men don't like brainy women.
Shirley You don't have to show you're brainy. You can always pretend.
Helen Will one of you help me with the tea?

Helen goes out. Shirley gets up and goes with her, leaving Judy and Saul

Judy How many girls have you slept with?
Saul (*startled*) What?
Judy You heard me. I've slept with four men so far. My theory is you can't know a man properly unless you've been to bed with him. Heard him cry out—you know. Though some men don't: they stay silent—you'd hardly know. Only when they just stop. Then you feel a fool. You ought to have noticed.
Saul Does Helen ...
Judy Oh no. Helen's keeping herself. Helen's a good girl. That is, Helen intends to sell herself in marriage to a nice man who'll keep her in comfort for the rest of her life. Marriage is legalized prostitution. Bernard Shaw said that. I hope I don't shock you. I think I'm more moral than Helen is, actually. And of course Shirley just wants a man to keep her in babies for the rest of her life. You haven't answered my question. How many girls have you slept with?
Saul Three.
Judy You can't despise me, then, can you.
Saul That's different. It's different for men: you know that quite well. But you don't shock me—and I don't despise you. I know I look rather conventional—but I do find what you say interesting. It's just a question of whether you plump for a quiet life or a dangerous one, isn't it. I think I want a quiet one.
Judy With Helen? You must be joking.
Saul She'd make a wonderful wife. An elegant hostess. I'm ambitious, you know. And I admire and respect Helen very much.
Judy You mean she's driving you mad with lust.
Saul I love her.
Judy You mean she's driving you mad with lust.
Saul Yes.
Judy It's her plan of campaign. One day someone will actually capitulate and propose. ... Any time you want to sleep with me, I'm available. I like men in suits. They seem so much more naked when they take them off.
Saul I hope my sister never behaves like you.
Judy Me, I'm just a mess. Everyone says so.

Shirley comes back from the—imagined—kitchen and sits down. Helen comes to the door

Helen Will one of you help me with the tea?

Judy gets up and goes with Helen, leaving Shirley with Saul

Shirley I can never think of anything to say to men.

Saul You just say what comes into your head.

Shirley Oh no. That might be boring. You have to present yourself, don't you. It's like putting on your make-up. Underneath the pancake I have quite a few spots. But you'd never know. I never go out without my girdle because my tummy might stick out. There now, you see, I forgot for a moment and said what came into my head. And what comes into my head is either too stupid, or too clever, or like just now, too rude. I hope I didn't shock you.

Saul Of course not. I may appear a rather boring and conventional person, but I am not easily shocked. Some girls do have tummies which stick out.

Shirley Are you quite comfortable? Would you like a cushion?

Saul Yes, I would. Thank you.

Shirley Helen's not very good at looking after people.

Saul I hope to be able to look after her.

Shirley Yes, isn't that odd. I'm one of the looker-afters, she's one of the looked-aftered. She's very beautiful. Do you love her very much?

Saul Yes.

Shirley I kind of get missed out.

Saul I find you very interesting to talk to.

Shirley That's one of the nicest things anyone's ever said to me. Do you think people are made for each other, or do you think it's all kind of chance? Is that a silly question?

Saul I think they're made for each other. My parents are made for each other. Although their marriage was arranged. Isn't that strange. Well more or less made for each other.

Shirley Quite a lot of my friends at school were Jewish.

Saul They liked each other, but it wasn't until after they were married that they fell in love. They're very close. They do everything for me and Stephen; I want them to be proud of me: which is more than he seems to do: but they do seem to, exclude him, in a way. There, I've told you more about myself than I've ever told Helen, in the three months I've known her.

Shirley But if you're a Jew are you allowed to marry someone who isn't Jewish?

Saul Not easily, no. It would upset my parents very much.

Shirley And her parents—well, the Jews! It's a disadvantage, isn't it. I know it shouldn't be, but it is.

Saul If two people love each other ...

Helen and Judy return with the tea

Helen I'm sorry it's so long. Judy broke the teapot. She's ever so clumsy. We've had to use a saucepan.

Judy It just all seems so boring to me.

Helen And the saucers are broken and the cups are chipped and ugly. If nobody minds I'm going off to bed.

Saul But Helen ...

Helen I've got a headache. I need my beauty sleep.

Saul But Helen ...
Helen Stop but-Helening me. I can't stand it. Good night.

Helen goes, bedroom-wards taking the tray

Judy (*following*) I've got an essay to write tomorrow. I can't stand all this socializing.

Judy goes, with the saucepan

Shirley Don't look so upset.
Saul Sometimes I think she hates me.
Shirley No. She's just rather bad-tempered. Well, she's pretty, isn't she. She's used to having things her own way. She's going to fail her exams. She doesn't do any work. Her parents wanted her to go to college: they thought she'd meet a nicer type of boy. They don't approve of Judy.
Saul I'm not surprised.
Shirley Judy's all talk. She's all right. And Helen's very loyal to her.
Saul You're very kind, aren't you. Will you come and sit beside me? I'd feel better if you did.
Shirley Who, me?
Saul Just for company. Helen wears me out. You've no idea. Her skin's so smooth—she's so near and yet so far. And her scent—I can't think; I can't work.
Shirley It must be terrible.
Saul You're pretty, too.
Shirley I don't seem to attract men. I think there's something wrong with me. Helen sends out a kind of aura. Do you think it's because I'm a virgin?
Saul So's Helen. Isn't she? Of course she is. I couldn't bear it if she wasn't. I'm so tired.
Shirley Lay your head on my shoulder. I wish I could do something for you.
Saul Kiss me.

They kiss

Shirley No-one's ever kissed me like that. Is that French kissing? Oh, do it again—no, don't don't, I mustn't, I want to, you'll despise me, supposing I had a baby, supposing you tell other people, anyway you're Helen's, oh please, not your hands, not there, oh what is happening to me—my mother trusts me, my father doesn't like me, really, he thinks I'm ugly and clever, Oh I love you, if I love you surely you love me, don't, don't, I'll have a baby ...

Helen and Judy stand in the door again with the tray and the saucepan

Judy I'm sorry we were so long with the tea. Helen broke the teapot.
Helen It was an ugly teapot anyway. Everything in this flat is cheap and ugly and chipped and boring. Fancy having to make tea in a saucepan. There must be some other way to live.
Saul I'm sorry if I'm a nuisance.
Helen It's terribly late, too. Tea always keeps me awake. I'm going to bed.

Saul Helen, please ...

Shirley Judy, I'm going to bed. I'm tired. Aren't you?

Helen I need my beauty sleep. I cut my finger on the teapot. Crawling round on the floor wiping up dust and tealeaves.

Saul But Helen ...

Helen Stop but-Helening me. You're so drippy. With your eyes and your clammy hands—I'm sorry. I'm sorry. I didn't mean ...

Judy I don't mind playing gooseberry.

Helen Shirley, there's nothing to be tactful about. I only asked him in for a cup of tea.

Shirley I'm sorry. I didn't mean—oh, I don't seem able to manage anything. I'm going to bed.

Shirley exits, in tears, with the saucepan

Helen Since you seem so fond of him, Judy, you look after him. Just don't offer him bacon for breakfast.

Helen exits, furious, with the teatray

Saul What's the matter with her?

Judy Sexual frustration. Same as you.

Saul Don't be so crude. It's different for girls.

Judy Not that I'd noticed. You're going to have to marry her before you drive each other mad.

Saul I can't marry her. I'm engaged to a girl in Canada.

Judy Now he tells us.

Saul A good Jewish girl filling up her bottom drawer with hand embroidered linen.

Judy Will they shave her hair off when she marries you?

Saul Yes. No. I don't know. I don't care.

Judy Do you love her?

Saul Yes. No. I used to. I didn't know, in those days.

Judy Know what?

Saul The ache. It is highly unsuitable for me to love Helen, but I do. She's bad-tempered, uncultured and unreasonable, and very stupid.

Judy I wouldn't say she was stupid. She's taking a degree with only half her mind upon it.

Saul That's stupid in itself. Supposing I do face my family, break my mother's heart—I'm the eldest son. Have you any idea what that means?

Judy What else did you have in mind? Do you just want to seduce her?

Saul I suppose so. What difference is it going to make to her? I just want to get through my exams. I love her. I don't love my fiancée. Who wants to marry someone they're in love with? It would be torment. She's driven me to prostitutes. I had to pay. Pay! It was horrible. Sex is meant to be a loving thing—an expression of feeling. You won't tell her. She'd be disgusted, wouldn't she.

Judy I expect she would.

Saul You too.

Judy No. I'm not disgusted. How much did you pay?

Saul Three pounds. A week's rent.
Judy I pay thirty shillings. I'll do it for that.
Saul What? When?
Judy Now.
Saul I can't. Where?
Judy Here.
Saul Someone might come in.
Judy I'll put chairs beneath the handles.
Saul You've done this before.
Judy I just get so sorry for Helen's young men.
Saul You're a whore. Helen's sharing with a whore.
Judy I think a financial transaction is morally superior to an emotional one. If I want any sexual experience at all, I have to choose between being labelled a whore or a cocktease.
Saul There are other alternatives.
Judy What?
Saul You could avoid pre-marital sex altogether.
Judy But I have to know. I'm too curious.
Saul Or get married.
Judy No-one's asked.
Saul I'm not surprised.
Judy Shall we begin? May I have my money first?
Saul Horrible!
Judy I do find you rather attractive, actually. I'd feel safer if we kept it strictly a matter of trade.
Saul I've only got twenty-five shillings left. Helen chose the lobster.
Judy That'll do.

Helen and Shirley stand in the kitchen doorway with the teatray and saucepan

Shirley I'm terribly sorry. I broke the teapot. And then Helen cut her finger . . .
Saul She didn't! Let me see . . .
Helen Leave me alone.
Saul But Helen.
Helen Do stop but-Helening me. I'm perfectly all right, apart from grovelling around in the dirt of that filthy boring kitchenette just so you can have your cup of tea.
Saul I'm sorry to have put you to the bother.
Helen It's ridiculous—tea at this hour. It will just keep everyone awake.
Shirley Nothing will keep me awake. I'm going to bed.
Helen You don't have to be tactful, Shirley. There is nothing to be tactful about.
Judy I'm going to bed too. I've got an essay to write.
Helen You're both trying to annoy me.
Judy You shouldn't always relate other people's activities to yourself, Helen. Some of them do have an independent existence.

Judy and Shirley exit

Helen I'm sure your mother never gives you tea from a saucepan. (*She gives him his tea*)

Saul No.

Helen Thick pile carpet from wall to wall: meals served by a maid at regular hours.

Saul Yes. But then when I see you I see the country vicarage, and the chestnut trees, bicycles cluttering up the hall, dogs, tea on the lawn ...

Helen Family quarrels, scenes, noise and neurotics ...

Saul Claustrophobia, for me. Schule, the Sabbath, Bar Mitzvahs—please let me kiss you.

Helen I wish they hadn't gone to bed. I knew you'd get silly.

Saul You're driving me mad. What's wrong with a kiss.

Helen Because one thing leads to another, that's why.

He kisses her. She allows further advances

Helen I told you one thing leads to another.

Saul But I love you. I'll always love you. You're the only girl I've ever loved. You're so beautiful—do you know how much money I've spent on you in the last three months? Eighty-two pounds, and my monthly allowance is fifty. I've borrowed it from my brother Stephen; I want to look at your breasts. My brother Stephen is an art student—he gets to look at women's breasts. You don't at architectural school. Only pediments and architraves ...

Helen You ought to get married—then you could do what you wanted.

Saul I can't get married for five more years, until I'm established—but I'll always love you. Please, Helen, let me ...

Helen Let you what?

Saul You know—don't tease me—you know what they call girls like you.

Helen All right, all right, all right ...

She capitulates. Then she disengages herself, and the scene goes back to before the die was cast

Saul Do you know how much money I've spent on you in the last three months? Eighty-two pounds, and my monthly allowance is fifty.

Helen I thought you liked my company—I didn't know you were trying to buy me.

Saul I didn't mean it like that. I was just trying to show how important you were to me.

Helen My body is, but what about me? What do you know about me? You've only taken me home once. You're ashamed of me.

Saul I'm not. I swear I'm not.

Helen You think more of your mother than you do of me. She hated me.

Saul I don't. She didn't.

Helen She did. You're a mother's boy. A little Jew boy. Anyway it's time you went. I'm tired and I want to go to bed. You've had your tea. Was it as disgusting as it looked?

Saul Yes. Helen, I love you; I don't care what you say, what names you call me.

Helen You don't show it. You only say it. If you had any pride you'd hit me for calling you names.

Saul I don't hit women ...

Helen (*recapitulating*) If you had any pride you'd hit me for calling you names.

He hits her. Helen collapses weeping. He folds her in his arms

Saul I'm sorry. I'm sorry. I don't know what's the matter with me. Well, I do. Helen, will you marry me?

Helen Yes.

Swift and merciful blackness obliterates the scene. In the darkness Helen and Saul take off the teatray and saucepan

The lights go up again, quickly. Stephen, Saul's younger brother, paces the flat and harangues Helen, Shirley and Judy

Stephen You must see it's impossible. It will destroy him. They'll never countenance his marriage to a goy ...

Helen Is that me?

Stephen Yes. They'll cut off his allowance. He won't be able to finish architectural school. He'll blame you for that for ever. I know my brother. It would be different for me, I'm an artist; I have renounced my Jewishness: the only God I recognize is the God of beauty: but Saul is Jewish to his heart strings—you've come along and twanged them for him, more or less by accident, but it's not the music of the spheres he's hearing.

Helen It's nothing to do with you.

Judy You're just worried. Somebody's got to be the good boy of the family and if it's not Saul it might have to be you.

Shirley They love each other. That's all that matters.

Stephen If it were me, and I was planning to marry a Muslim Eskimo, that's all that would matter. But it's not me, it's Saul.

Helen Did he send you round to say all this?

Stephen No. You know he's already engaged?

Helen What?

Stephen A nice orthodox girl, currently in Canada. Wedding preparations are underway.

Helen You're making it up.

Stephen I've brought the press cutting from the *Jewish Chronicle*.

Helen exits weeping. Shirley follows to comfort her

Judy I don't think I would have the courage to interfere so with the course of events.

Stephen No? Well, you're a woman. You should take the passive role. You must see, it's a ridiculous marriage. She's trapped him into it.

Judy Not at all. He can't wait to marry an Anglican parson's daughter.

Stephen You're Judy, aren't you. He talked about you. The available one.

Judy Not to everyone.

Stephen Ask and you shall be given. Seek and you shall receive. Are you available to me?

Judy Yes.

Stephen I thought so. What is it about me?

Judy You're such a bastard. You send tremors up and down my spine. Touch me, and it seems like something destined ...

Helen and Shirley come back into the room.

Stephen re-sets the scene

Stephen Saul is already engaged to a nice orthodox girl, currently in Canada. Wedding preparations are underway.

Helen What a tone of triumph! I know that. He told me. But he doesn't love her. It was imposed upon him. And they'd never cut off his allowance, and anyway he has a trust fund in his name they can't touch. Now I am going to choose bridesmaids' hats for my wedding. My father is marrying us in his church: if your stupid religion won't accept me, I'm sure mine will accept him.

Judy Accept anyone these days.

Shirley He's giving up everything. It's true love.

Stephen Judaism? A stupid religion? My poor brother.

Helen exits, accompanied by Judy

I managed that badly. I'm very tactless.

Shirley If it's what you feel, it's as well that you said it.

Stephen Do you think so? People don't seem to like me much. Most of the time it doesn't matter, because I don't like them much either; sometimes it does. I would like you to like me.

Shirley I do. You frighten me rather. You make me feel such a little girl.

Stephen I expect she just wants to get out of this dump.

Shirley I do my best to keep it tidy. Helen spends her time at her dressing table, and Judy at her desk; I'm rather boring—I love cleaning, actually, and cooking.

Stephen A Martha in a world of Marys. As it should be.

Shirley You have a button off your shirt. Would you like me to sew it on for you?

Stephen Yes. If you will personally take off my shirt.

She does so. They embrace, falling bedwards

Stephen I seem to have an extraordinary knack with women. I'm not at all nice to them, and have no trouble getting them. Saul is a polite, serious, civilized person and has to either marry or pay. I don't understand it. Well, I do. There is no justice in the world, and one's success, in realms of both art and sex, bears ample witness to that fact.

Night and silence fall. The lights fade

The Lights come up again as Babel reasserts itself. It is 1960. There is a noise, off, of babbling toddlers and wailing infants. Helen and Shirley sit sipping tea

Helen Doulton. Do you like it?

Shirley Better than making tea in a saucepan.

Helen Those dreadful days. Don't talk of them. (*Shouting*) Nanny, can't you keep those bloody children quiet?

Silence falls

Helen Do you think she has a gag?

Shirley (*alarmed*) You'd know. Wouldn't you?

Helen You seem to get more serious with the years, Shirley.

Shirley The formative years are so very important. The child suffers terribly from separation from the mother. If one is going to trust one's children to somebody else, one should at least know ...

Helen I suffer terribly if I am not separated from my children; I have equal rights, surely, with them.

Shirley No. One renounces those the moment one conceives. Can I have some more tea? Stephen doesn't allow tea in the house.

Helen What do you mean, doesn't allow?

Shirley It's a stimulant.

Helen He drinks, doesn't he?

Shirley Alcohol. Not tannin. The tannin in tea lines the stomach with a thick brown coating which prevents the absorbtion of Vitamin B.

Helen Vitamin B is absorbed by the gut, not the stomach. Of course Stephen only went to art school—one must expect him to be ignorant. But I'm surprised at you, Shirley.

Shirley Stephen knows best about most things.

Helen Does he?

Shirley Yes. I was so ignorant until I married him. You've no idea.

Helen I thought you had a degree, like me.

Shirley I mean about important things. Like art, and cooking and herbs, and garlic, and jazz; and the rearing of children, and what a man is, and what a woman is ...

Helen You don't mind his infidelities.

Shirley He is completely, totally faithful to me. I am his wife. I am the mother of his four children ...

Helen But he sleeps with his models, Shirley. All London knows he sleeps with his models.

Shirley That's art. You wouldn't understand. Artists aren't like other men. I don't care what he does: I love him. I will wash for him, clean for him, wait up for him, go hungry for him.

Helen What? Is that necessary? At five hundred quid a painting?

Shirley I did. I went hungry. I worked my fingers to the bone, charring, all through the fifties, so we could pay the studio rent, so he could buy pigment and canvases—

Helen —and beer ...

Shirley I still have a cough from those days. I think it's nervous, really. I love him and he loves me.

Helen He's mad. Everyone knows he's mad. I can see that being married to such a doormat must drive him mad.

Shirley I'm not a doormat, I'm a wife. And in all the days of our hardship, when he was struggling for recognition, you and Saul didn't help one bit.

Helen We had our own troubles. Jack and Marie cut off his allowance. They didn't cut off Stephen's. Saul was very upset. He had to make his own way; went into property and owes his prosperity to no-one but himself. And when Jack and Marie come to dinner, I give them Parma ham followed by veal in cream sauce.

Shirley Saul was the eldest son. Different things were expected. And Stephen always did so much for Saul.

Helen Like trying to stop him marrying me?

Shirley He was right.

Helen Thank you.

Shirley You're hard and heartless. You married for money, not love. I'm sorry to say this, but you're not a natural mother.

Helen Why are you so angry? I'm not. (*Recapitulating*) Vitamin B is absorbed in the gut, not the stomach. Of course Stephen only went to art school; one must expect him to be ignorant. But I'm surprised at you, Shirley.

Shirley I surprise myself. Do you think I've got very stupid?

Helen Yes. Cabbagy.

Shirley What am I going to do?

Helen Leave him. He's unfaithful, he humiliates you in public ...

Shirley At least he tells me. He doesn't pretend.

Helen He uses you, in every possible way; he always has.

Shirley He's an artist.

Helen Artist-schmartist.

Shirley Where would I go? How would I live? He wouldn't give me a penny. He'd fight a divorce. I can't earn. I'm not trained to do anything. I thought I might be a teacher—but I'm too old to be trained. If I had one child I could get a job as a living-in domestic, but not four. Besides, they need their father. They love him. I love him, Helen.

Helen You mean you have no alternative but to love him.

Shirley You live such a shallow existence. You have no idea what love is, or how misery tangles itself in the heart and becomes part of it. You have your children by Caesarean—

Helen It does leave a scar. They said it wouldn't show but it did—both times ...

Shirley —and have them brought up by nannies—I'm sorry but you're not a natural mother.

Helen Why does that make you so angry. I'm not angry.

They stare at each other, puzzled, having reached the same end by different routes

Judy enters

Judy I've come for help.

Helen You look terrible. No-one's worn their hair like that for years.

Judy Haven't they? I've been too busy to notice.

Helen A woman's first duty is to look after her looks.

Judy Who said so?

Helen Saul. What sort of help? Are you pregnant?

Judy Yes.

Helen Now how did you let that happen?
Judy I was drunk. So was he. He does drink. I keep him company.
Shirley That's very unwise. Stephen drinks, but I never do. Someone has to drive home. You know what it's like. Those parties at which the men drink, and the women stand about waiting and yawning, and worrying about the baby-sitter, and if they say anything get accused of being wet blankets.
Judy I don't have a baby-sitter, and I don't stand about, I drink, and his wife drives home.
Helen What is it you want? The name of an abortionist?
Judy I have the name. I need the money.
Helen Money. Don't you have any? You have a career. Don't you? What was it you were doing? I forget.
Judy I work for the B.B.C.
Shirley I told you what would happen, if you took a shorthand typing course on top of a degree. You'd be such a good secretary they'd keep you one for ever. I suppose young men from Oxford just come in and get promoted over your head.
Judy Yes. And in all these years I don't think I've taken one letter I couldn't have written myself—or recorded any decision I couldn't have taken myself.
Shirley At least I have something to show for the years.
Judy I've been offered a job as A.S.M. in television. I can't be pregnant. Not now.
Helen Do we know the father?
Judy Jonathan. He used to be a friend of Stephen's.
Helen The anaesthetist! He was old even then. Dandruffy. You can't love him.
Judy We console each other.
Helen You need consolation?
Shirley Of course she does. She leads an empty life. Pursuing sex down sordid alleys.
Helen If he's in the medical profession, why do you need money?
Judy Abortion is against his principles.
Helen But not letting his patients die, from drunken negligence.
Judy He was cleared at the inquest. It was never proved.
Helen I wish I could let you have the money, Judy, but I can't. Saul keeps very strict accounts. He doesn't mind how much I spend—but he is very particular about what I spend the money on.
Judy You could lose it. A couple of hundred between the coats and the curtains and the nannies.
Helen I could. But I wouldn't. I have a morality, you know. My father was a clergyman.
Judy It's nothing to do with morality. It's spite.
Helen Do you think so? You may be right. It often comes to the same thing, I admit.
Judy You're trapped here in your sterile marriage. Nothing but money. You hate Saul; you hate your children—you hate yourself.
Helen At least I defuzz my legs. I pluck the hairs out one by one, with tweezers.

Shirley You don't! Where do you find the time?
Helen I delegate. I organize.
Judy You don't care about me. Either of you.
Helen Friendship is a matter of trade, I think. We don't get much in return.
Judy Tell Saul it's for me. He'll want to help.
Helen No. He won't. I only see you because Saul disapproves. We have
nothing in common any more.
Judy Shirley, Stephen would want to help me.
Shirley No. He wouldn't.
Judy Why not?
Shirley Girls who are anyone's are no-one's responsibility. Besides, we're so
in debt. There's nothing to spare.
Judy You wouldn't think so, from the gossip columns.
Shirley Stephen has to socialize. A fashionable painter does.
Judy I remember how he talked about art, beauty, and freedom. How he
feared the pollution of the market place. What have you done to him?
Shirley We have a mortgage and four children. That's reality.
Helen No. That's your reality. Not his. You're very boring, Shirley. Lend
her the money. You can. I can't.
Judy Doesn't that humiliate you, Helen?
Helen No.

Judy turns on her heels, goes, then re-enters

Judy I've come for help.
Shirley We knew you would, sooner or later.
Judy You were right and I was wrong. I'm left with nothing, except the
memory of a few good lays and more humiliations than I can remember.
Helen You look dreadful. If you smartened yourself up a bit—you could at
least try sleeping your way to the top.
Judy You could do that. I can't. My eyes fill with tears. I make scenes. Now
I'm pregnant, by a married man I don't love. A child needs a mother and
father. I can't provide one. I want the money for an abortion. A proper
one, hygienic, with an anaesthetic. I'm frightened of pain, and dying. And
prison. I know a girl—the abortion went wrong. She had to go to hospital
—they *waited* at her bedside until she was better. Then she went to prison.
Shirley There's no-one else you can turn to?
Judy No.
Helen You've slept with too many husbands, I suppose.
Judy Yes.
Shirley The trouble is, if you give yourself to everyone, you're no-one's
responsibility. It's very difficult in this world to find anyone to really care
about you. If it comes to your interest or theirs, theirs comes first. I suppose
my parents care about me. I care about my children.
Judy You care about Stephen.
Shirley He can make me unhappy, if that's what you mean. Most of the time
I wish he was dead.
Judy Don't say that. I don't wish that of anyone.
Shirley I do. Lots of people.

Helen I don't expect anyone to care for me. I don't care very much for anyone. I like to have a good time. I sometimes wish I could be swept away by love. The days begin to seem a little bit the same.

Judy You might be. I live in the hope that one day, one night, more likely, the man in bed beside me will realize how much I have given him. What I am offering. It's not just my body—but it's all they seem prepared to take.

Helen I'll try and raise some money. I might even ask Saul. I think he used to rather like you. Though he pretended to be shocked.

Shirley Yes. Please you do it, Helen. It upsets me. I don't want to be part of it. It feels like murder to me. And yet I see it must be done. There must be some point to life except just splitting, reproducing; every time I get pregnant I know I'm putting something off. But I don't know what. I'm a good wife. I try to be a good wife.

Helen I try to have a good time.

Judy I just feel sick.

Shirley Come with me. Camomile tea, sipped slowly is a great help. I remind myself sometimes, of my mother. She died, you know.

Judy I'm sorry.

Shirley She sacrificed everything for me. So I could get to college, get my degree. I don't know if she liked Stephen. She never said. But then I never asked. There are some questions in family life which can't be asked. Do you like my husband, mother. Or how many times have you been unfaithful to me, since we were married. One longs to know, but dare not ask. Perhaps you are right, not to be married.

Judy and Shirley leave, passing Saul on the way: he nods curtly

Saul Yak yak yackety yak. The girls again. What are they beefing about this time?

Helen Judy's pregnant.

Saul Did it the right way, did she, for once.

Helen You've become rather crude.

Saul You might say I'd been driven to it.

Helen You might say, frigid wives were caused by boring husbands.

Saul I think I'd better make another entrance.

Helen Yes. I think you have.

Saul goes back to the door, and makes another entrance

Saul Darling, you look lovelier than ever.

Helen Thank you. How was your day at the office?

Saul We've got the plans for a tower block through. Thirty stories. Eight months it's taken us. We're using a new light-weight aggregate—they've given us the go ahead. But that's too technical for you, isn't it.

Helen Yes. It is a little, darling. Would you like a drink? Gin?

Saul Thanks. What a lucky man I am! When Beefy Burger comes I'll tell him all about it. Mind you, news travels fast.

Helen Time was when one offered Planning Officers pheasant and claret—now it's Beefy Burger and his like, and steak and chips washed down by Scotch.

His wife wears low-cut dresses with sequins and sweats under her armpits.
He fingers her in public.
Saul There's a lot to finger. I understand the temptation.
Helen Oh? If I put on a pound, you complain.
Saul You live by style, my dear. Mrs Burger lives by the flesh. Which is just
as well, because otherwise he'd squash the life out of her.
Helen I'm glad you're in a good mood. I have a favour to ask.
Saul Money?
Helen In a way.
Saul Nothing is money in a way. Everything is money. Time is money. Love
is money. Marriage is money. Parents are money, giving or taking. Look
after the money and life looks after itself. Our children have no money
sense. Can't you do something about that? Do you think it's their nanny?
Perhaps if you took more of a personal interest? I'm sure you have a proper
sense of the value of things. I bought Nina a talking doll from the USA.
and Samuel a tank made in West Germany and they just grabbed them at
the door and ran off upstairs, without so much as a kiss or a smile. They're
not grateful, Helen.
Helen I tell them to be grateful.
Saul How can they be grateful if you're not grateful?
Helen I am grateful.
Saul You don't show it.
Helen I run this house. I talk to your boring business contacts, I bear your
children, I diet on your behalf, I ask you how you got on at the office. What
more do you want?
Saul Warmth.
Helen I don't make chicken soup for you, I admit. Neither do I crowd you,
smother, reproach you, wait up for you, ask you where you've been, cripple
you with guilt, or have hysterics night and day. I am not your mother, in
other words.
Saul Yes, why don't you ask me where I've been? Shirley asks Stephen where
he's been.

Helen shrugs

We sleep in twin beds. It's unnatural.
Helen It's hygienic and practical. I am not one for body smells. If you want
the double bed back, it's in the attic. I'll arrange to have it brought back
down to the bedroom.
Saul How much did you say?
Helen Two hundred pounds.
Saul I'll leave a cheque on the hall table tomorrow morning.
Helen Or perhaps a little more?
Saul We'll see what kind of mood I'm in.
Helen Very well—I don't make chicken soup for you, I admit. Neither do I
crowd you, smother, reproach you, wait up for you, ask you where you've
been, cripple you with guilt or have hysterics night and day. I am not a
Jewish mother. I am not a Jewish wife.
Saul More's the pity.

Helen Why? What do you want me to do? Go with you to synagogue and listen to you thanking God you weren't born a woman?

Saul I haven't set foot in a synagogue since I married you: on the other hand I have daily thanked God I was not born like you.

Helen I don't think a Jew is in any position to despise anyone male or female.

Saul I don't suppose you do. The English middle classes are amazing. Antisemitism runs in the blood.

Helen I'm not middle. I'm upper-middle.

Saul While you're slumming down here in the ghetto, however, you're not above asking for money. What's it for?

Helen Never mind.

Saul I do mind. I have a right to know. It can't be an abortion. Not of any child of mine, at any rate. But perhaps you have a lover? Someone uncircumcised, more your kind?

Helen I've changed my mind. I don't want your money, Saul. I'd rather do without. It is not worth the bother of asking. I am tired of selling my body and soul in exchange for it.

Saul Other women don't sell, they give. But that is beyond your comprehension, I daresay.

The Lights fade to darkness, then come up again to the bright lights of the Riviera. It is 1964. Helen and Stephen are unobtrusively sunbathing. Shirley sits at an English pub table

Judy enters in a bikini, trailed by Jonathan—hairy legs in Bermuda shorts

Jonathan He is my son. He needs a father.

Judy I am his father, and his mother.

Jonathan But I want to look after you.

Judy Look after your wife. You have two children already.

Jonathan Girls.

Judy Why do you have to spoil this holiday? Shirley asked *me*; she didn't ask you.

Jonathan Stephen asked me. Old times and all that. I knew you'd be here.

Judy All the way to the South of France. Saul's insurance against a rainy day. Two acres and a vineyard and a prime building site. He doesn't even keep his mistresses here. He has no time for mistresses, not these days.

Jonathan I need you, Judy.

Judy Do you? I don't need you. Time was when I did. Not now.

Jonathan I admire you.

Judy I admire myself. I'm doing all right. I have a flat, a good job, prospects, a child, an *au pair* to look after it, boy-friends as and when I want. No-one's socks to wash—no-one to make me feel guilty.

Jonathan You must be lonely.

Judy No. I have everything I want.

Jonathan You're too self-sufficient. It isn't good for you. You're brittle. You'll crack. Women should bend; they should be pliable.

Judy Should! I'm doing all right.

Jonathan I'm not. I drink too much. I can't go on like this. I'm not happy with Rosemary.

Judy That's not my fault.

Jonathan Yes it is. You made me dissatisfied. You're the mother of my son. I want to make amends.

Judy No you don't. You're bored with your life. You want a change.

Jonathan Other women would have had hysterics, had an abortion, kicked up a fuss. You went ahead and had the child. Our child. It was then I realized you were a serious person.

Judy Thank you.

Jonathan You've been twice as beautiful since.

Judy If I'm serious, why do you never talk to me about serious things?

Jonathan What things?

Judy Politics, power, principles.

Jonathan Don't I?

Judy No. When you want to please, you discuss my character or my looks. Otherwise you talk about yourself. Shall we swim?

Jonathan I can't swim.

Judy Paddle, then.

Jonathan If you want me to leave Rosemary, I will. Careful, there's a jellyfish. They sting, you know.

Judy I don't need looking after, Jonathan. I am perfectly capable of looking after myself. I don't want to be your nurse and nanny, and stand between you and the whisky bottle for the rest of my life because one day one of your million or so sperms swam up and met one of my ova, and wham, there was Benjy.

Jonathan It was meant. Everything's meant.

Judy It's all chance, Jonathan. There is no God. When you administer nitrogen instead of oxygen because the tubes are wrongly fixed by a technician who'd had a bad night, is that the hand of God or the laws of chance?

Jonathan I give up. I'll go home tomorrow. I tried to make amends. I could have made you happy.

Judy I am happy.

Jonathan No.

Judy Shall we swim?

Jonathan I can't swim.

Judy Paddle then.

Jonathan If you want me to leave Rosemary I will.

Judy shrieks and hops about the stage in pain and panic

Jonathan What's the matter?

Judy I've trodden on a jellyfish. I think it's a Portuguese man-o'-war. I shall die. Help me. Please help me. People die!

Jonathan Not from jellyfish. It's uncomfortable but not dangerous.

Judy You've no idea! Nobody cares. I could die and nobody would care. What would happen to Benjy if anything happened to me? Who'd look after him? He might have to go into a home. I can't afford to be ill. I can't afford to take a day off work. I'll lose my job. You don't seem to realize how alone I am. It's all your fault. You wouldn't help. He's never had anyone but me . . .

Jonathan Marry me. Rosemary doesn't need me. You do.

Judy Yes. Yes.

Jonathan Come back to the villa, my love. There's a first aid cupboard in Helen's bathroom.

Judy It will be empty.

Judy and Jonathan exit

Helen and Stephen sit up

Helen What's the matter with him? He has a perfectly nice wife.

Stephen So have I.

Helen I know.

Stephen That's my trouble, of course. She uses me like a stud to father her children. She uses me as a martyr uses the Inquisitor, to further her progress towards God. She means to be the patron saint of suffering womankind. I see her washing the lipstick stains from my shirts, grim faced, red eyed. She says nothing. She washes my brushes; brings my models cups of tea, suffers in silence when I complain about the size of her tits. She sucks me dry, If it wasn't for her I'd be a passable artist. I don't want to live the way I do. I hate every minute of it. Lying on this God-awful fashionable beach every summer.

Helen Then why do you come?

Stephen Because I feel guilt.

Helen So you should.

Stephen Doing this with me doesn't make you feel guilty? She is your best friend.

Helen It's one of the rules: boy-friends take precedence over woman-friends. We all acknowledge it.

Stephen Women frighten me. By God, they frighten me. The female in pursuit of the male. After his cock, his money, his house, his life.

Helen How else are we to live? Why didn't you want me to marry Saul?

Stephen You were a cold, mean bitch and he was a cold, mean man. I wanted you for myself. I only had Shirley because I couldn't have you.

Helen You married her. You ought to be loyal to her.

Stephen I'd rather be married to you.

Helen No thanks.

Stephen What's wrong with me?

Helen I wouldn't want to see the look on Shirley's face. Or on her childrens, come to that. I'm tanned on my front but not on my back. Rub more sun-oil in, if you please.

Helen lies down. He rubs. Presently he lies down as well

Jonathan wanders back, searching for something. Judy peers anxiously after him

Judy It's a blue flip-flop. Hurry. Supposing the poison gets into my blood-stream?

Jonathan Here it is.

Judy and Jonathan exit

Stephen and Helen sit up

Helen What's the matter with him? He has a perfectly nice wife.
Stephen So have I.
Helen No. Shirley's not nice. She uses you to further her maternal purposes.
Stephen You don't think she's my victim?
Helen Of course not.
Stephen She thinks she is.
Helen She loves every minute of it. Lipstick stains upon your collar, vomit on the carpet, broken window panes, pictures in the Sunday papers. Martyrdom! Danger, artist at work.
Stephen Artist. I'm not an artist. What am I going to do? I'm a hack. I've sold out.
Helen I know.
Stephen Do you really? What a relief.
Helen You're all life style, no life. A fucking disgrace.
Stephen You even swear.
Helen What's it all about, anyway? Your vision of the universe, pure or sullied. Mud-pies! Men are such children. Come and look, what a lovely mud-pie I've made. In tune with all creation. While Shirley cleans the brushes and brings you and your mistresses early morning tea in bed. I'd kill you.
Stephen Kiss me again. I'm going to go mad. You know Saul is ruining this beach? I can hear the throb of bulldozers in my ears. Your villa will soon be lost in a sea of concrete hotels, each one taller than the next.
Helen From the tallest, on a clear day, he might see the shores of Israel.
Stephen A physical impossibility.
Helen He wouldn't give his life. But he'll give money. And since money means more to him than life—why did you try to stop me marrying him?
Stephen Because you're a cold bitch. And I had a vision of your clammy children, holding out their hands for more, and wished to spare the world.
Helen You were right. And yours?
Stephen Noisy, dirty and loving. I warn you, I love them.
Helen By our children you shall know us.
Stephen Shall we run off together?
Helen Never.
Stephen Because of Shirley?
Helen Don't be ridiculous.
Stephen I might even be faithful to you.
Helen Why? You'd get no sexual satisfaction from me, I'm a cold bitch. Everyone knows.
Stephen I'd soon put an end to that.
Helen How?
Stephen I'll show you.
Helen What, here? I've got a headache and I hate sand.

Stephen slaps her. Helen cries

Helen No-one's ever done that to me before.
Stephen You'll do what you're told.
Helen All right.

They sink down behind their sand-dune

Saul enters and carries his glass and scotch egg over to where Shirley sits

Shirley Your tan's fading. Fancy us meeting like this. I'm so seldom in London. I just have this dentist in Knightsbridge. I usually go to the Kardomah, but it was so full. I thought, well, times are changing, ladies are allowed in pubs, and who should I meet but you. My teeth are in a shocking state. Stress, the dentist says. But that's just a fashionable thing to say, isn't it. How can what you feel in your heart affect what happens to your teeth?
Saul I have almost perfect teeth.
Shirley So I see.
Saul I very rarely lunch here. I very rarely leave the office at all. Quite a coincidence, our meeting.
Shirley I hope you don't mind being seen with me. Your country cousin. Your dowdy sister-in-law.
Saul You always look very nice, Shirley. Feminine.
Shirley It was a wonderful holiday, wasn't it.
Saul Was it? It was work for me.
Shirley You work so hard. You could afford to work less hard. You must be so rich.
Saul I certainly make the tax-man rich.
Shirley And the whole Mediterranean bristles with your achievements.
Saul Sewage is a local government responsibility, not mine.
Shirley I didn't mention sewage. I think you must have a conscience, Saul.
Saul What about?
Shirley If you worked less hard ...
Saul Why should I?
Shirley You'd have more time to spend with your family.
Saul Who? Me? I'd be in the way. I'm just the all purpose provider. The children think I'm an idiot, and Helen thinks I'm a nuisance. I'm used to it by now. Why, has Helen been complaining?
Shirley No. On the contrary.
Saul You see? If she had a different nature—but she's self-sufficient, self-contained. She doesn't like men: she doesn't like sex. I adore her. She has a finer nature than me. She's a bad-tempered bitch but I need her, and she needs me. Like you and Stephen.
Shirley I begin to wonder.
Saul No. Don't wonder. Just be loyal. He'll grow out of it.
Shirley Picasso never did.
Saul Stephen's no Picasso.
Shirley You underrate him. You always have. It's why ...
Saul Why what?

Shirley Well, you know what he's like about you. And yours. The only reason he married me, I sometimes think, is because you slept with me, and he mistook an evening's episode for something more serious.

Saul It wasn't an episode, for me. It was serious. But it was too nice. I needed something dreadful, like Helen. Still do. I wish I didn't. We could have been happy, Shirley.

Shirley You're a faithful man.

Saul Yes. And you're a loyal wife, and that's the way it must stay. It's a kind of superstition with me—if I don't play around with anyone, neither will Helen.

Shirley And mine is, if I don't make a fuss, Stephen will come back. And that's what I want. At least, I think it is. So let's forget it, shall we? I hope you don't mind being seen with me, your country cousin. Your dowdy sister-in-law.

Saul You always look very nice, Shirley. Maternal.

Shirley (*after a pause; hurt*) It was a wonderful holiday, wasn't it

Saul Was it? It was work for me.

Shirley Helen certainly enjoyed it.

Saul I expect she did. It cost enough.

Shirley She enjoyed the company.

Saul Family? That's not like her.

Shirley No. It's not. Is it. Though of course I was a friend before I became family. I used to think people felt loyalty to their friends when they didn't feel it for their family. Perhaps neither is true. It was quite an eventful holiday.

Saul Was it?

Shirley Yes. And Judy trod on a jellyfish and decided to marry Jonathan.

Saul I hardly imagine that's why she decided to marry Jonathan.

Shirley No?

Saul Any girl in her position would marry, if asked. Especially if asked by the father of her child. Alleged. Still, I suppose a girl has to name someone. Girl! She must have been all of thirty. Getting desperate. Settle for anything, even someone else's husband.

Shirley I think she married him because she trod on a jellyfish. Life can be very arbitrary. You can intend and intend all you wish, but the die fall this way or that.

Saul It's arbitrary only if you let it be. You control your own destiny. Well, perhaps women don't. Men certainly do. I'm sure I do.

Shirley You think one should interfere, in the workings of fate?

Saul Most certainly.

Shirley You don't like Judy, do you.

Saul I don't approve of her as a friend for Helen. No.

Shirley Why not?

Saul She's an easy lay.

Shirley Did you ever sleep with her?

Saul Who didn't?

Shirley That doesn't make you feel warm towards her, or pleased when you think of her?

Saul No.

Shirley You slept with me.

Saul Are you sure?

Shirley Don't you remember?

Saul I'm sorry—I sowed my wild oats like anyone else.

Shirley I expect you were thinking of Helen, at the time.

Saul I always think of Helen.

Shirley She's not nice. She isn't.

Saul I know that. What difference does it make?

Shirley It isn't fair.

Saul Of course not.

Shirley You're so smug.

Saul No. But I think I am fortunate, to have loved only one woman in my life.

Shirley Not like your brother.

Saul He plays around. Well, you knew that when you married him. But he always comes back.

Shirley And I'm supposed just to sit it out? Until he's too old? I might have to wait for ever. Picasso was never too old. I'm afraid artists wear well.

Saul You can hardly put Stephen in the same category as Picasso.

Shirley No. I don't. Not any more. And where does that leave me? Giving everything for nothing. This time I think he is going to leave. Unless someone does something. And you have to do something. That's why fate brought us here together. It must be a million to one chance.

Saul Well, no. Not if your dentist and my office are both in Knightsbridge, and the Kardomah's full and my coffee dispensing machine has jammed. Do something about Stephen? I have no influence with him at all. I'm sorry.

Shirley Do something about Helen.

Saul What has Helen got to do with Stephen?

Shirley Everything.

Saul When? Where?

Shirley You're not at your home. I'm not at my home. So I expect they're together now. It's her mid-cycle, isn't it. He wants to give her a baby. He wants to bring her to life, as you haven't. He sees her as a challenge. He told me so. You'd be surprised what I know about your wife's erogenous zones, menstrual cycle and so on. He tells me everything. It makes him feel better. He doesn't like deceit.

Saul In your house?

Shirley No. In yours.

Saul Mine?

Shirley Whenever possible. He likes it. He's very envious of you. He always wants what's yours. He married me because you slept with me, so he thought I must be worth something. He enjoys Helen twice as much because he's in your bed in your place. The elder son. I don't care about the whys. I just want him back. You can kill Helen for all I care, but leave Stephen. He doesn't love her. He's just bored and doesn't know what to paint next, or what to do for an encore. Perhaps I shouldn't have told you. I didn't mean to. It's dangerous to push things—bring them to a confrontation. I don't care what you say: life's better left arbitrary. It might just all blow over. It might.

Saul goes to the door

Come back—please come back

   Saul exits

(*moving after him*) Forget I said anything. Please. Pretend it hasn't happened. Please don't go.

Saul reappears for a minute: stands silent. Then he goes

   Please!

But it is no use. Saul has gone

CURTAIN

ACT II

Judy sits disconsolately. Jonathan enters, shaving his right cheek

Judy My mother died.

Jonathan I'm sorry. Well, it was expected.

Judy She didn't expect it. She didn't expect to be knocked down by a bus on the way to post Benjy his seventh birthday present.

Jonathan She died the happier because you were wearing a wedding ring.

Judy I am tormented by if only's. If only she'd forgotten his birthday, if only she'd looked instead of just stepping out.

Jonathan You might as well say if only he hadn't been born. But he was meant to be. He fought his way through unlikely odds in order to be born.

Judy You're so rational about everything else, and so romantic about children. I have to be rational about them: I have to feed them and clear up after them—I've no time to be romantic.

Jonathan It seems to irritate you if I'm fanciful.

Judy Yes. I don't know why.

Jonathan You must be feeling low. I'll take you out to dinner tonight.

Judy Where?

Jonathan The *King's Head*? They do good steaks.

Judy Yes. Thanks. If only I'd been with her when she died.

Jonathan If someone's in a coma, for four weeks, can't speak or hear or see, there isn't much point. In effect, she died four weeks ago.

Judy She did come out of it for a time, the nurses said. But that was when I had to be at the school. Benjy's open day, after all. His reading's still not very good. And he still wets the bed. Do you think I'm too smothering?

Jonathan I think you've turned into a good and conscientious mother. Making up for the first early years. Poor little boy: he'll settle soon enough. When's the funeral?

Judy Saturday.

Jonathan I'm on duty. I would be!

Judy You can't bear funerals anyway, can you. What about the big children? Rosalind's putting them on the train on Saturday morning. Someone will have to meet them. Or perhaps she could keep them, just for the morning. She wouldn't surely go to Court again because I have to go to my mother's funeral. Would she?

Jonathan Quite possibly.

Judy I understand why she resents me—I just hadn't expected it to go on for so many years. She seems to imagine you're made of money—she doesn't understand what we have to go without so she can be kept in comfort, or

what long hours you have to work. You don't think I should go out to
work? We do need the money.

Jonathan No. Benjy needs you.

Judy He's seven. At school.

Jonathan What about holidays, when he gets ill—when he gets home from
school?

Judy I could get an *au pair* . . .

Jonathan He needs his mother. Do you want a stranger in the house, taking
over your rôle?

Judy No.

Jonathan I might fancy her rotten. It's always happening. Some young foreign
bird.

Judy I know.

Jonathan Besides, what you'd have to pay out in tax and wages and having
Bengy properly taken care of would be more than you could ever earn.

Judy I suppose you're right. But I need to earn.

Jonathan Not much. You didn't do all that well as a career girl. And you
weren't happy.

Judy How do you know?

Jonathan From the way you used to sleep around.

Judy Is that a symptom of unhappiness?

Jonathan Yes. We're happy as we are. I'm tired when I come home. I need
comfort and peace and security and the knowledge that you're here looking
after everything.

Judy I suppose you're right.

Jonathan What more important work can a woman have than being a good
wife and mother?

Judy What more important work can a man have than being a good husband
and father?

Jonathan Now don't get all smart-alecky. He has to be a provider too. Alas.

Judy Yes but if I was working . . . Oh, what's the use. I don't know what's
the matter with me. Perhaps it's the pill, making me depressed. It does, you
know. I don't care what they say.

Jonathan Imagination. Hardly scientific. I'm a doctor, Judy, I do know. I'll
be working late again tonight.

Judy Poor darling.

Jonathan What's that smell?

Judy It must be the milk boiling over. I'm sorry.

Jonathan You're so inefficient. Such a muddler. It's as well you've got me to
look after you.

Judy I know.

Jonathan Most men wouldn't put up with it.

Judy I'm sorry.

Jonathan Never mind. I'll go.

Jonathan goes

Judy continues to sit disconsolately

Jonathan enters, shaving his left cheek

Judy My mother died.

Jonathan I'm sorry. Well, it was expected.

Judy She didn't expect it. She didn't expect to be knocked down by a bus on the way to post Benjy his seventh birthday present.

Jonathan She died the happier because you were wearing a wedding ring.

Judy She would have died happier still if I'd been to visit her yesterday.

Jonathan You couldn't. It was Benjy's open day. You had to go to that.

Judy Just about the time she came out of the coma, the nurses said. After that it was useless.

Jonathan Quite. If someone can't hear or speak or see, what is the point of sitting beside their bed. Cheer up, my dear. I'll take you out to dinner tonight.

Judy Where?

Jonathan What about the *King's Head*?

Judy That's not a restaurant, that's a pub.

Jonathan They do very good steaks.

Judy You could have gone to Benjy's open day.

Jonathan How? I was on duty.

Judy You could have got out of it. You have in the past.

Jonathan You're his mother. He needs you. He's insecure enough as it is.

Judy What do you mean, insecure?

Jonathan He wets the bed.

Judy Lots of children wet the bed.

Jonathan Lots of children have mothers who go out to work, when they should be staying at home, but that doesn't mean it's a good thing.

Judy Shirley's children are in a much better state since she started work. So's she, come to that.

Jonathan That's necessity, not choice. Look, Benjy had a bad enough start in life. You left him with minders for the first year—that's the most crucial time. The least you can do is make it up to him now. Besides, you've nothing better to do, have you? Do you grudge him your time? If you do, you should never have had him in the first place.

Judy It was your doing, too.

Jonathan In these days of the pill, my dear, it is hardly the man's responsibility to avoid conception. Is it?

Judy It makes me depressed. I don't like taking it.

Jonathan It's imagination. Not scientific. But then women don't think like men. Just as well, or what a boring world it would be. Don't let's argue, not today. I know you're upset. Unless of course arguing makes you feel better. I don't mind. I'm used to it.

Judy Will you be coming to the funeral?

Jonathan You know I can't stand funerals. When is it?

Judy Saturday.

Jonathan But the children are coming on Saturday. And I'm on duty.

Judy Your first wife can surely look after her children for one morning, to let me go to my mother's funeral.

Jonathan It will set a precedent. She'll have us back in the Courts.

Judy Then let her.

Jonathan You must have some sort of responsibility towards the children, Judy. You did break up their home, after all.

Judy I know. All the same ...

Jonathan I work my guts out to keep two homes going. All you can ever suggest is that I take time off work to do what is clearly your responsibility. Put in an appearance at your own child's school, meet them off trains, and cook their dinner. Is it too much to ask?

Judy You could spend less time in the pub.

Jonathan God, you're a monster. Why did I ever have anything to do with you? I do my best to be nice to you, to keep you calm—you're a millstone round my neck.

Judy I think I should go out to work. I can't stand about here listening to all this.

Jonathan Over my dead body. I would rather die than see another generation of children ruined. What's that I smell?

Judy The milk boiling over.

Jonathan You are so inefficient. When you did go out to work, did you get promotion? Could you even keep yourself?

Judy No.

Jonathan Shorthand-type! What an ambition! You mean to sacrifice us all, the children's happiness, my comfort, our marriage, so you can shorthand-type for some executive idiot.

Judy No. Not really. I expect I've forgotten how to do that too.

Jonathan Unless of course it's the executive idiot you're after.

Judy What do you mean?

Jonathan You must find all this fidelity very boring, after the life you were used to. Though God knows what you do when I'm not around.

Judy God knows. You could always come home from the pub and find out.

Jonathan Where are you going?

Judy To take the milk off the stove. Where else?

Jonathan I'll do it. You'll only put the pan down on the table and leave a ring.

Judy Probably. All the same, I'm going out to work.

Jonathan Over my dead body.

Judy Die, then.

Judy exits, Jonathan follows. Helen enters, painting her nails, followed by Stephen, with a newspaper

Stephen My country is at war.

Helen Your country?

Stephen Israel.

Helen Oh yes. That. I hope it doesn't lead to trouble.

Stephen Lead to trouble?

Helen Well, if other more important nations become involved, it might get serious.

Stephen You don't think this is serious? That Israel might be annihilated? Swept into the sea?

Helen The Jews always make such a fuss.

Stephen You're intolerable.

Helen I'm sorry. I thought you'd stopped being a Jew. There doesn't seem much point in it, any more. If you think you're Jewish you go and live in Israel, if you think you're English or American, or whatever, you stay where you are and join in.

Stephen Sometimes I think I was better off with Shirley.

Helen Sometimes I think I was better off with Saul. I preferred him by day; I prefer you by night. He was away by day, most of the time. You're away by night, quite a lot. One clearly never gets what one wants.

Stephen That's because you only get out of life what you put into it. And you put in nothing.

Helen I think you ought to go and fight for Israel.

Stephen I can't even fire a gun.

Helen You could set free some bus-driver who could.

Stephen Me? Drive a bus?

Helen Why not? You can only paint three paintings a year. You're owned by a gallery. They buy in any of your paintings which drift back on to the market. They keep up your prices artificially.

Stephen How nicely you put it.

Helen You complain non-stop about how this country is castrating you: how there's nothing to fight for, nothing to achieve, no purpose in your life. I think you should go. Your passport's got another year on it. It's in the top left dresser drawer.

Stephen You want to get rid of me.

Helen You're just under my feet all day. At least Saul was out most of the time.

Stephen You wouldn't care if I were killed.

Helen You could always be the bus-conductor, not the driver.

Stephen I shan't give you the satisfaction.

Helen Is Saul going off to war?

Stephen Why do you care what he does?

Helen I don't care. I'm just interested. That's all that keeps me alive, really. Wanting to know what happens next. Leaving you was the making of Shirley—she looks wonderful.

Stephen How do you know?

Helen I met her for lunch.

Stephen But she hates you. She has every reason to hate you.

Helen No. On the contrary.

Stephen At least Saul has enough dignity to hate my guts.

Helen But he's not going off to war?

Stephen No. He was all talk. He's making too much money. He's the scum on the surface of this rotten society.

Helen Stephen, do go off and save Israel. Please, for all our sakes. You might come back a different man ...

Stephen starts to go

Where are you going?

Stephen There's a new receptionist at the gallery. All of eighteen and more than willing. I flatter her. She has a high opinion of me.

Helen She's not married to you. Judy's having an affair with the office boy in her Department. He's seventeen.

Stephen She's disgusting.

Helen Yes. I think so, too.

Stephen What sort of wife are you?

Helen Confused, mostly. Different husbands seem to expect such different things. Have a nice time.

Stephen goes

Helen waits

Stephen returns

Stephen My country is at war.

Helen Your country?

Stephen Israel.

Helen I knew it existed in your heart. Not its reality, you must get confused. Nothing could live up to the dream, I imagine.

Stephen You're so English. I suppose you want the Arabs to win. The noble Bedouin. Living in his filth, with the flies eating away at this children's eyesight.

Helen Yes. The hygiene argument.

Stephen You are determined to be provocative. You don't seem to realize this is serious. Israel might be annihilated—swept into the sea.

Helen There's nothing you can do about it.

Stephen I could go over. Join up.

Helen Why? You haven't been to a synagogue for years. There's nothing Jewish about you at all.

Stephen What do you know of suffering, enduring, hoping.

Helen What do you?

Stephen It's bred into me, as anti-semitism is into you.

Helen I used to get all that from Saul. I didn't expect it from you.

Stephen Saul talked. I felt. I'm wasting my time here. This country cripples me. I can't talk, I can't think, I can't paint.

Helen That has nothing to do with where you are, just what you are.

Stephen I'm growing fat and lazy and old. You won't take in my mother. How am I going to feel when she's in an old people's home?

Helen Much the same as you do now. Relieved at not having to see her every day.

Stephen You're callous.

Helen First she cast off Saul for marrying me, and then me for marrying you. Never satisfied.

Stephen She came to love Shirley. She understood Shirley. You were something too strange for her. She solved her problems with chicken soup and cucumber sandwiches, the way Shirley did.

Helen She never uttered a civil word to me. Now she can't speak because she's had a stroke it all seems much the same. Let her go and live with Shirley.

Stephen If I went to Israel now she would be pleased and proud.
Helen And you'd be a few thousand miles from reality.
Stephen That is reality. Desert, danger, gun-fire. Real life. Real death.
Helen But you can't fire a gun.
Stephen I could set someone free who could. At least I could do something: I wouldn't feel so impotent.
Helen What you're saying is, if I don't agree to have your mother living with us, in other words if I don't take her over on your behalf, you're going off to fight for Israel?
Stephen I am saying nothing of the sort. I am trying to explain to you that I am worthless to you, and worthless to myself. What sort of husband do I make you. I'm always in bed with someone else. What sort of father? I let Shirley take the children and didn't move a finger to stop it. What kind of painter? I paint for money, nothing else. I have nothing left to say. At least let me be a good Jew. (*He hunts in the dresser drawer*)
Helen What are you looking for?
Stephen My passport. It was in the dresser drawer.
Helen I sent it off for renewal. Well, mine was due. It should be back in a few days.

Stephen starts to go

Where are you going?
Stephen Never mind.
Helen It's the new girl at the gallery, isn't it.
Stephen Why should I hide it? Yes.
Helen There'll be nothing left, soon. Sex is all we ever had.
Stephen (*going back to the drawer*) Somehow, the spark's gone.
Helen What are you looking for?
Stephen My passport. It was in the dresser drawer.
Helen I sent it off for renewal.
Stephen Liar. It wasn't due for renewal.
Helen I sent it off with mine, which was. It saved postage.
Stephen When did you ever think about postage? Where is it?
Helen Please don't.
Stephen You can't condemn me to live like this, half alive.
Helen Darling ...
Stephen You've never called me darling.
Helen You'll be killed if you go.
Stephen It's the kind of thing which happens.
Helen Your passport's in the bedroom. Are you really going?
Stephen Yes.
Helen Good lord.

Stephen goes

Helen finishes her nails, and then puts on a very large and becoming black hat

Shirley enters

Shirley My poor orphaned children.

Helen You might think of me. I'm a widow.

Shirley You make a very good widow. The title enriches you. It gives you a depth, people might otherwise feel was lacking.

Helen As for your children, they are quite accustomed to being fatherless. A dead father is often less embarrassing than a living one, and I am sure you are so supremely adequate, Shirley, as to make up for any possible loss they feel. There was no insurance policy, you know. Nothing for me.

Shirley I should hope not. I would hate to think he'd been paying life insurance for you, while failing to provide maintenance for his children. It's not as if you even made him happy.

Helen Was I meant to?

Shirley Yes. I don't think you even loved him.

Helen The sex was good.

Shirley You could have had that without breaking up my marriage. Everybody else did.

Helen I daresay I would have, if you hadn't gone running to Saul and upset him.

Shirley There comes a time when you have to take your life in your own hands and act.

Helen It doesn't seem to turn out much better if you do. You'd have done better just to drift along, as usual. That particular act led to two divorces, one death, and five children with broken homes. Assuming of course, that marriage is better than divorce; an unbroken home preferably to a broken one, and life better than death.

Shirley You must think so!

Helen I'm not sure, any more. Stephen certainly wasn't. Men are allowed to have these doubts. Well, they can afford to, so long as there are life forces like you around, Shirley.

Shirley You injured me.

Helen It seemed important at the time. A passion greater than myself. Happiness arising, phoenix-like from the ashes of other people's hopes. Then it just flew off, somewhere else.

Shirley Do you think we change? Any of us?

Helen No.

Shirley Then what's the point?

Helen I have no idea. A cosmic game of chance—we're rattled around like dice, cast out, picked up, rattled again. It gives me terrible headaches, sometimes. They've planted a tree to Stephen, in Israel.

Shirley Now listen. If they water it, it will grow. If they don't, it won't. You left your children to be brought up by nannies . . .

Helen Well, I never liked them. Little stick creatures with runny noses—they were the worst of me and the worst of Saul. At least yours seemed to be the best of you two when they were little, at any rate; and as for Judy's Benjy, I'm sure he wasn't Jonathan's at all.

Shirley I am trying to say something. Daily dealing with children gives one a very clear sense of reality, and of cause and effect. It's what you lack, Helen. If you wash their bottoms, they don't get nappy rash. If you forget,

even for one day, they do. You are too fanciful, Helen. Of course I went to
Saul about you and Stephen. Why should you get away with it? If you
didn't want it to happen, you could just have said no, Stephen, you're
married to my best friend.

Helen You do pride yourself.

Shirley All our misfortunes are due to bad temper and lack of responsibility
and nothing to do with fate, or cosmic dice. It is simply the last thing said,
which finally provokes one to action.

Helen In that case you should learn to hold your tongue.

Shirley I shall learn something. I shall wrest some meaning out of life, if it
kills me.

Judy enters

Judy I want help.

Helen We seem to have been here before.

Shirley Yes, but we were younger then.

Helen What difference does that make?

Shirley We had more energy.

Helen Speak for yourself. I have been careful to let no-one sap mine. And I
have never washed my face with water, so my complexion remains good.

Judy Please!

Helen You're looking quite dreadful, Judy.

Judy I am having a dreadful time. Jonathan is divorcing me, for mental
cruelty.

Helen Really? Is it possible? Would he notice?

Judy My going out to work, he says, amounts to cruelty.

Helen Is it worth it? All that aggro for a weekly pay packet?

Judy Monthly. It is my right! He's claiming custody of Benjy or I wouldn't
care. He says I'm unfit. I should never have married him. All that's happened is that I've lost years seniority. I'm going to have to start as a secretary again. And for what? For the privilege of having cooked that drunk's
dinner for five years, and gone without heaven knows how many good lays.

Shirley No. I don't think you were cut out for marriage.

Judy I want you to stand up in Court and say I'm a good mother.

Shirley Are you?

Judy It's irrelevant. It's a matter of principle.

Shirley You're even turning into a man. Men are always citing principle as
the reason they do things they want, and don't do things they don't want.
They're irresponsible. They father children and then they'll do anything,
cripple themselves in factories, put themselves in prison, invent enemies
and stand in front of their guns, rather than put up with the boredom of
actually living with their progeny. I see the whole male world, capitalism,
communism, religion, war, as the flight from washing up, wives, children
and reality. And you're a fool to wish to join it, Judy. And I shan't say
you're a good mother, Judy, because you're not. Of course office life is
preferable to running a home, but that's not the point. Poor little Benjy.
Has he stopped wetting the bed?

Judy No. He's a heavy sleeper.

Shirley He'd need to be, I imagine.
Judy Benjy is your responsibility ...
Shirley How?
Judy If you'd helped me, last time I asked, he wouldn't exist.
Shirley From Benjy's point of view, that seems an argument for not helping you. I will not help you. I don't want to help you. I don't feel like helping you.
Judy I never did you any harm.
Shirley Yes, you did. You devalued me, you mocked me, you despised me for years. Stupid Shirley, following her own nature! Housewife! Hoist by her own petard—abandoned by her husband—insulted by her children.
Helen (*interested*) Do they?
Shirley Yes. Rude ungrateful brats. What I made them. I had no existence of my own. I was just a bridge between two generations—a female body plagued by a mind I did my best to ignore.
Judy You could do something now—all kinds of opportunities are opening up.
Shirley What? Teachers' Training? Open University? No thanks. My life ends with the menopause. I shall shrivel up and die as soon as possible. I feel my breast for lumps every day, hoping to find them.

Shirley exits

Judy Come back.

Shirley reappears

Shirley No. That's that.

Shirley exits, definitely, for once

Helen I find that disconcerting. I can only be one sort of person because she's another.
Judy You'll help me, then.
Helen What, stand up in Court and say you're a good mother?
Judy Yes.
Helen It depends what you mean by a good mother. I think I'm a good mother: I abandoned my children. I didn't want them to see the light of dislike and the glimmer of boredom in my maternal eye. I sacrificed a lot to do it: Saul's love and the good opinion of the world.
Judy It was better when you simply were, and didn't try to justify yourself. You did what you wanted, as always.
Helen Didn't you?
Judy No. I wanted true love, like anyone else. I wanted soft kisses and moonlight and adoration, but I wasn't born to inspire it. All I could do was lie on my back and open my legs, and hope some spark would leap from me to them and ignite an undying passion.
Helen Did it?
Judy It lit something up in Jonathan, but I think it was only whisky fumes.
Helen And you thought you would make him happy, and he'd never drink again.

Judy No. That didn't enter my head. I thought he might make me happy.
Helen I married Saul because he said it would make him happy.
Judy The becauses are a delusion. There are so many.
Helen What do we do now?
Judy You stand up in Court and say I'm a good mother.
Helen Why?
Judy Because it's like a murder with no motive—it has no precedent, because you simply do it, and feel better for it.
Helen Like fucking?
Judy Speak for yourself. Mine are all motive: Shirley's are all consequence. Help me. Do it.
Helen Very well.

Judy and Helen exit

The Lights fade to a BLACKOUT. *It is 1973*

Saul and Jonathan enter into the darkness. Saul searches for a light switch

Saul I can't find the light switch. It's the beginning of the end. Everything's collapsing. It's the end of capitalism: the end of civilization.
Jonathan I can't see where I'm going.
Saul Then stay where you are.
Jonathan I need a drink.
Saul Who doesn't. You know I'm going to have to sell this house to pay off the bank? My fault, I used to be froth, now I'm scum. At least you doctors preserved a clear conscience.
Jonathan Uh?
Saul I'm lucky not to be in prison. You know those Christmas cases of whisky I used to give? They weren't an expression of gratitude, my lawyer now says. They were bribes. I've had to take the children out of school. I've even considered marrying the *au pair*; cheaper than paying her. A pity I can't marry my lawyer. I daresay by this time next year it will be legal. Where is the bloody thing?
Jonathan It's June and it's snowing.
Saul I know, I know. Even the seasons are topsy-turvy. And the nations too. The Arabs are taking over. Stephen died in vain.
Jonathan I heard he didn't die in action. He was driving a bus. He put his foot on the accelerator, and not the brake, and went into an irrigation canal. Drowned himself and two passengers.
Saul You heard that, did you?
Jonathan Yes.
Saul Who from? My ex-wife?
Jonathan His widow.
Saul She would. Damned lie. I've found the switch but there's still no light. I can't have paid the bill.
Jonathan Perhaps there's a power cut.
Saul No. Never is. The bank has never made a mistake, there's never as much money as you thought, and essential services don't work because you haven't paid the bill, not for technological reasons. New lessons for the

middle-classes. Impoverished. The workers are doing all right. The revolution is upon us. We non-productive bastards are going to suffer from now on. And serve us right. The weavers of dreams and the builders of parking lots.

Jonathan What are you so cheerful about? Where's the drink?

Saul I am liberated. I am punished. Here, a Christmas candle, left by the Swedish *au pair* before last. There is no drink. I have no money. Can you lend me some? (*He lights the candle*)

Jonathan No.

Saul I thought you'd say that. A few certainties are left in life.

Jonathan You've changed, since Stephen died.

Saul I can now allow myself a few irresponsibilities, I daresay.

Jonathan If I had money to lend you, I would.

Saul They all say that. I seem to remember saying it myself, in the days when I was rich.

Jonathan I ruined myself, trying to save Benjy from his cow of a mother.

Saul I always rather thought Benjy might be mine.

Jonathan What did you say?

Saul. Helen was such a frigid bitch, in those days. Though I do hear she's changed. If we'd married different women, do you think we'd have ended up the same, pretty much the same, or not the same at all? Studies on identical twins indicate a man's earning potential is genetically determined, not influenced by environmental factors at all.

Jonathan You're trying to upset me.

Saul No more than you, telling me my brother died in an irrigation ditch, when I assumed he was a hero, dying to relieve me of my responsibilities.

Jonathan I was only repeating what Helen said to me.

Saul Where were you? In bed with her?

Jonathan Certainly not. So far as I can see, your wife is having a lesbian relationship with my wife.

Saul Paranoia.

Jonathan I see no other explanation for it.

Saul They're friends.

Jonathan Women don't have friends. Not like men. I want you to take back what you said about Benjy.

Saul It's said now. It can't be unsaid. I rather wish he wasn't mine. A child of fifteen, still wetting the bed!

Jonathan I told her. I warned her. Of course he's mine.

Saul Does it matter one way or another? A child that's named yours is as good as yours.

Jonathan No! All that struggle, that misery; the sacrifice, financial ruination, solicitors' letters—not my son? The whole point was: he was my son.

Saul Point? I don't understand you. There is no point. Activity is its own reward. Sexual, uxorious, paternal, professional? It's a long time since I saw a point. I see no point in spending my life perfecting my skills as an architect, in order to be unemployed when I reach my peak—to see my best buildings labelled anti-social by ecological fools and sociological morons—in the end, not to be able to pay my own electricity bill! Point?

In pouring love into the cracked vessel you call a wife? In caring for children
who turn out to be not your children at all, whatever their genes, but just
more people? No point.

Jonathan Benjy was the point of my life. Benjy meant everything to me. I
left my first wife and daughters for him: put up with Judy for years. I
wanted him to have the chances I never had: the choices I went without.
I wanted him to be myself, perfected. Do you really not have a drink?

Saul I could give you a cup of tea, but I'm ashamed of the cracked cups.
We used to have a Doulton tea-service but I threw it at Helen the day I
discovered she was having it off with my brother Stephen.

Jonathan Whores and bitches.

Saul If you'd married Shirley—if I'd married Shirley. But whoever wanted to
marry Shirley? Where are you going?

Jonathan Home.

Saul You have no home.

Jonathan My long home. What else is left for me? Look at me. A dirty old
drunk with two failed marriages, my breath stinking from a rotten liver,
you've taken away my only son. The drink's run out. Look at me, I say.

Saul The light's too dim.

Jonathan Take me seriously.

Saul Never have. Never will. As we were born, and so on. You're a shmuck.
Takes a woman to take a shmuck seriously.

Jonathan starts to go

No, look, don't go.

Jonathan You've said it all.

Saul Not like this. It's been a long time.

Jonathan (*going*) Pills, I suppose, or an injection.

Saul Come back.

Jonathan (*returning*) Finality frightens people.

Saul You're a useful member of society. I'm not. I'm not killing myself.

Jonathan (*going*) You're not a shmuck.

Saul I daresay I could find a drink.

Jonathan exits

Of course Bengy could have been Stephen's, not mine. You know what
Judy was like. It seemed to matter once. He won't do it. People don't.
Nobody I know at any rate. People who say they will, don't.

Saul follows Jonathan out

*The candle blows out, then the Lights come up. It is 1977. Shirley and Judy are
sitting in the flat, reading*

*Saul and Helen appear. He is taking her home to the flat she shares with
Shirley and Judy*

Judy is ethnic, Shirley gay, Helen much as usual

Saul Can't I come in?

Helen No. Nostalgia can go too far.

Saul Not even for coffee?
Helen Certainly not for coffee. Gold-dust, these days. Judy won't have it in the flat, anyway. Bad for the karma. She's into the mystic East, you know.
Saul Please. Let me come in.
Helen And of course Shirley won't have a man in the flat. She's into lesbianism.
Saul Jesus!
Helen Who? One has to be into something. One has to have some occupation. You know you ought to know that. Are you a good social worker?
Saul It depends how you define your terms. Let me come in to the warm, Helen.
Helen You have to be fresh for your clients, tomorrow. But thank you for dinner.
Saul A treat for me, too. I usually use the Chinese take-away.
Helen I'm surprised the children don't ask you over.
Saul I'm not. At least kiss me. You have lovely breasts.
Helen Have I? Still?
Saul Yes.
Helen Well, I never breast fed. What we look like isn't supposed to matter, of course.
Saul It does. It does. Supremely.
Helen You paunchy, smelly, balding old man, then. You disgust me. Animal. Lecher. (*She goes inside the flat*)

He hammers on the door. Helen emerges again. They kiss

Saul Can't I come in?
Helen No.
Saul Not even for coffee?
Helen Certainly not for coffee. Like gold-dust. Judy won't have it in the house. Or alcohol, of course. She attributes Jonathan's suicide to whisky.
Saul She doesn't think it had anything to do with her?
Helen Of course not. Shirley's gone gay: did you know.
Saul You?
Helen Not my scene. A cop-out, if you ask me. Of course she always liked softness.
Saul I'd like to see them both again. Let me in.
Helen I don't think we have anything in common, anymore.
Saul A certain intimacy, one way or another.
Helen All of it purely accidental.

Helen goes inside the flat. Shirley and Judy look up from their books. Helen goes outside again, and kisses Saul

Saul Can't I come in?
Helen The past is over. It has nothing to do with the present. We're different people.
Saul I still love you.
Helen Love? What's love?

Saul I'll show you.
Helen You always said that, but you never did. Your brother showed me
    more.
Saul I won't reproach you for that.
Helen I should hope not. I won't reproach you for Shirley and Judy.
Saul I only ever cared about you. After you left everything went wrong.
Helen For me too. Was it us stepping out of line, or just us getting older?
Saul Both.
Helen I'm sorry I went with Stephen. I only did it to upset you. Because you
    were away so much.
Saul Liar.
Helen Liar yourself. Come in.

Helen lets Saul in. Judy and Helen look up

Saul Hello, Judy. Hello, Shirley.
Judy Hello, Saul.
Shirley Hello, Saul.

CURTAIN

FURNITURE AND PROPERTY LIST
(See production note p. iv)

ACT I

On stage: FLAT AREA:
4 chairs
Sofa
Table. *On it:* 2 books (for **Judy** and **Shirley**)
Bed
Cradle
Dresser. *On it:* candle in candlestick, matches. *In cupboard:* Martini, sherry, glasses

ELSEWHERE:
Beach umbrella
English pub table
2 chairs

Off stage: Tray with 4 chipped teacups, saucers, teaspoons, sugar bowl, milk jug (**Helen**)
Saucepan with tea (**Judy**)
Bottle of sun-oil (**Helen**)
Drink and scotch egg (**Saul**)

ACT II

Strike: Beach umbrella
Pub table and chairs
Any used glasses

Off stage: Electric battery razor (**Jonathan**)
Newspaper (**Stephen**)
2 books (**Shirley, Judy**)

Personal: **Helen:** nail polish

LIGHTING PLOT

Property fittings required: nil
A flat, and elsewhere

ACT I

To open: Lighting full up on flat area

ACT II

To open: As Cue 1

EFFECTS PLOT

ACT I

Cue 1   Lights come up after **Stephen**'s line: "... bears ample witness to that fact"   (Page 9)
Sounds of babbling toddlers and wailing infants

Cue 2   **Helen:** "... keep those bloody children quiet?"   (Page 10)
Cut off sounds

Printed in Great Britain by Butler & Tanner Ltd, Frome and London